The SOTAI Method

Japanese Exercises to Correct Body Imbalances

操体

JOHN DIXON

Table of Contents

Introduction

Sotai is a system of exercises created by a medical doctor in Japan called Keizo Hashimoto in the twentieth century. Hashimoto became aware that the standard medical treatment he practiced had limitations and was not always effective in resolving the health issues of his patients, especially for orthopaedic problems. This led him to study other traditional systems of medicine. Over time, he developed his own system of body correction known as sotai.

A key principle behind sotai is that our bodies have been created and designed in a way for us to be healthy and happy. However, when we live contrary to this natural design, sickness and unhappiness follows. Sotai is a method to bring our body back in tune with this natural design.

This book contains a select number of basic sotai exercises, which can be easily carried out at home and takes around ten to fifteen minutes to perform. Sotai is not an exercise system that builds large muscles or strength or has a goal of increasing flexibility. The objective of sotai is body alignment and correction.

It should be explained that sotai is a therapy in which a person can receive treatment from a sotai practitioner to help correct their body imbalances. However, sotai is also an exercise therapy that can be carried out by individuals wishing to correct their own physical distortions. This book only shows the sotai exercises that individuals can carry out by themselves.

Part I

Chapter One: The Origins of Sotai

Portrayal of Keizo Hashimoto as a young man

Dr Keizo Hashimoto (橋本敬三, 1897-1993) was born in Fukushima prefecture in Japan. He became a doctor of Western medicine and at age 38 was sent to war in North Korea as an army doctor. He was captured by the Soviets and interned in Siberia. After the war, he returned to Japan in 1948.

Christianity was influential in Hashimoto's early life. He had a Protestant upbringing and attended church until going to war as an army doctor. However, there were aspects of Christianity, which apparently troubled Hashimoto, particularly on the issues of sex and salvation. In later years, it seems that he adopted the Buddhist philosophy of karma and other Japanese spiritual concepts into his own personal beliefs.

The origin of sotai

Hashimoto was convinced that "*man is originally healthy, but that sickness starts when the body structure develops deformation*". He formulated the concepts of sotai from working fifty years as a medical professional in Japan.

As a doctor, Hashimoto noticed that his treatment was not effective for orthopaedic problems such as knee and back pain. His patients often went to acupuncture or bone setters (bone manipulation therapies) for relief. This led him to learn from other systems of traditional medicine, such as acupuncture, massage and bone setting (similar to osteopathy). After his return from war, Hashimoto taught in an acupuncture department.

Hashimoto was familiar with another system of natural medicine at the time, called seitai jutsu. This is a method where movement is made in an easy and comfortable direction for a few seconds and then relaxed. This method allows for the alleviation and correction of some bodily problems. Seitai jutsu could be said to be the origin of sotai. However sotai went on to develop differently. Sotai places some emphasis on the patient performing an active movement with analysis of the ease or dis-ease of each movement to discover imbalances, rather than the focus being on the therapist alone making the movement and assessing the imbalance themselves.

Hashimoto observed that some of the techniques from other traditional medical systems involved reducing pain by moving a body part in the direction that is unpainful. This technique was to be a major concept in the sotai exercise system - to move the muscle or joint in the direction that is easy or feels comfortable.

Another factor he recognised is that if stimulation is given to a muscle or acupuncture point which feels comfortable, such as rubbing or massaging an acupuncture point, this can help heal the person. This is the case even if bones are out of alignment, because as the soft tissue muscle connects with the bones, the stimulation given to a comfortable point in the muscle will help to correct the misalignment. He concluded that all Oriental medicine systems had the same goal of correcting deformations in the muscles, bones and tissues, even though their methodology may differ. With his increasing knowledge helped by his frequent access to patients, he was able to try out his techniques and theories with good results, even on people who would normally have to undergo surgery.

According to Hashimoto, sotai is as simple as '*asking the patient if the movement feels good?*' If it feels good, the patient will get better. The sensation of '*good*', can be interpreted as a feeling of pleasure or release. The Japanese have an expression for this – "*kimochi-ii*", which a person utters when they feel good or a strong sense of relief after bodily discomfort. It simple means '*that feels great*'. However, this is not the same pleasurable feeling that a person gets from eating cake. It is more a feeling that something feels fundamentally *right* in the body.

Portrayal of Keizo Hashimoto in his later years

In the last part of his career, Hashimoto wrote many articles discussing his theories. For the most part he received little attention. However, finally in the 1970s, the media started to pay attention to his work. His effective treatment for a young boy with muscular dystrophy was broadcast on NHK, the largest TV network in Japan, which led to an increased interest in his method. He gave many lectures around Japan. Before Hashimoto passed away, he stated that '*sotai belongs to everyone*'.

The meaning of sotai

操体

The name sotai (操体), is a reversal of the Japanese word '*taiso*' (体操), meaning exercise. Sotai is made up of two words. The 'so' in sotai, means *manipulation*, particularly the *manipulation* and awareness of bodily movement that feels *right*, gives relief and encourages healing. The word '*tai*' refers to the body, physique, health or frame. Sotai can be literally translated as '*the right way to move or manipulate the body*'.

Chapter Two: The Principles of Sotai

Fallen man and bodily imbalances

As a Christian, Hashimoto would have been familiar with the Biblical statement from the book of Genesis, that man was made in the image of God. It was logical for Hashimoto to consider - did God intend for us to be so badly designed that we fall sick and require other men to fix our sicknesses? Hashimoto did not think so. He wrote: "*Health is not a miracle. Health is the state Nature (God) planned for us and this should be achieved in a comfortable way*[1]". Similarly, as God is said to have given free will to man, man also has free will in determining his choices and habits which impact on his health. Hashimoto hypothesised that man is sick because he does not know the right condition to maintain health. Instead he pursues a life that brings him closer to disease.

Eastern medicine considers that a cause of disease is that of imbalance or deformation in the body. Traditional arts such as acupuncture, anma massage, shiatsu or bone setting have been used for centuries to correct imbalances. In Japan, a patient attending an acupuncture clinic should not be too impatient for a resolution to their problem. In some cases, they are encouraged to attend treatments for several weeks. It must be understood that a body goes out of balance and becomes sick over a long period of time. Correcting a body that is out of balance takes a period of time also. However, in the West, the idea of waiting for healing is an alien concept. We expect quick results. A painkiller can get rid of a headache in twenty minutes. However, this quick relief won't lead us to correct the imbalances that caused the headache in the first place such as a lack of sleep, improper foods and drinks or stress. This quick fix enables us to carry on as before. However, by not correcting the subtle imbalances, we slowly undermine our overall health.

According to Hashimoto, the cause of sickness is due to faulty ways of living, particularly in four key areas. These are - breathing, eating, movement and mind. If the way we live is contrary and disruptive to the natural design of our body, we can become sick. Fortunately, our body has a self-correction ability and we can use sotai to support this process.

Some key principles underlying Hashimoto's sotai system are:

- Deformation and imbalances in the body system cause disease.
- These occur due to living contrary to the four principles of life.
- Sotai seeks to correct deformation and imbalances by carrying out movements of the body in the direction that gives relief and comfort.

Chapter Three: Sotai Theory

The structure of the body is relatable to the structure of a building. The difference being that man is a moving building. To support the upright stance of man, the foundation must be firm but to allow movement, there must be flexibility and movability in the joints. As all parts of the body interact with each other to move, there must be unity and balance between them. For example, when making movements, such as bending the upper body to the right, the natural way is to shift the weight of the lower legs and hips to the opposite side - the left, in order to make the movement balanced. If we go against the natural movement by bending to the right and putting our weight on the right side then the movement is unnatural and hindered and we can create structural imbalances.

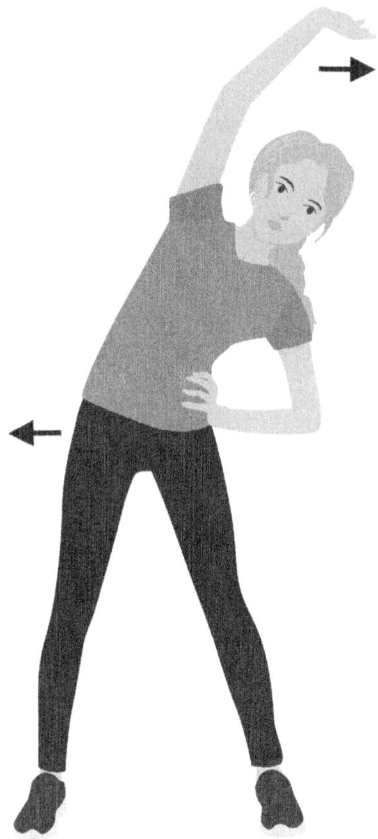

If we bend the upper body in one direction, the weight in the lower body distributes in the opposite direction to create balance.

As an upright being, our centre of balance and base of movement comes from the hips, waist and spine. Many problems stem from deformities in these areas. Our upright nature also causes us to be more at risk of issues of the back and spine. Our spine is the fundamental structure and skeletal frame of the body and can be misaligned from excess tension caused by misuse of the muscles pulling upon the spine abnormally. As the spine is a major passageway of our autonomous nervous system, problems related to the nervous system can also be caused. Certain therapies such as chiropractic medicine, recognise that subluxations in the spine (misaligned vertebrae) can cause various ailments and seek to manipulate the vertebrae back into their correct position.

Sickness is the body's message

Sotai encourages us to learn to live in tune with the body and respect it. For example, if we are injured, the simple message the body gives us is to stop and rest. The message is so simple yet a person might drag themselves to a therapist hoping to speed a recovery. This is unnecessary. The body wants you to rest, so rest.

It may seem a strange concept that imbalances in the body are in fact a natural process rather than an unnatural one. Imbalances can be seen as bodily adaptations to an unnatural situation or habit, to attempt to regain some kind of balance and enable the body to keep functioning. It is only when these mal-adaptations become excessive, that they begin to show the signs of manifesting as disease.

To give an example, a child is under a continual state of stress, perhaps due to a home situation or a stressful situation at school. Consequently, the child adapts to the pressure by applying tension, such as tightening the abdomen or shoulders or grinding the teeth. This body armour enables the child to protect themselves and absorb some of the pressure to survive the stress. Unfortunately, if the level of stress continues or intensifies, eventually the hardened musculature will impact on the efficiency of the internal organs. Such a child may develop digestive problems or other nervous conditions. These patterns may also become fixed. Emotionally, they may hold repressed anger or fear, which may manifest in various ways later on.

Chapter Four: The Four Principles of Life

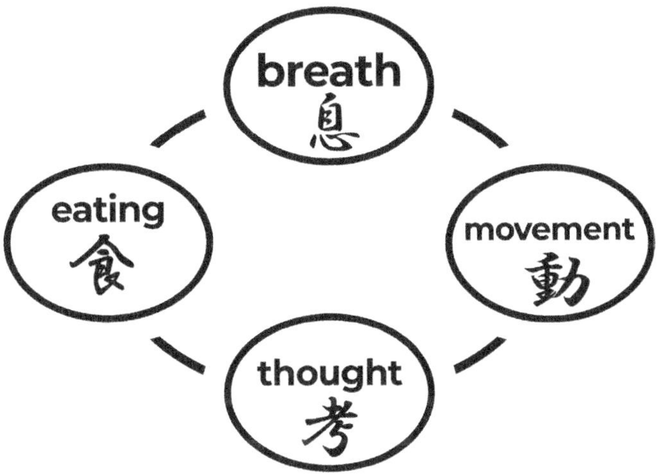

The sotai way is to encourage reconnection with the natural principles of life. These principles are breath, eating, movement and correct thought.

Breathing

Hashimoto promoted the importance of breathing as one of his four sotai principles. With his Christian influences, he would have been aware of the book of Genesis and God's creation of Adam – "*then the Lord God formed the man of dust from the ground and breathed into his nostrils the breath of life, and the man became a living creature*".

The way we breathe indicates our state of health. The deeper a person's breathing pattern, the more healthier they are. Shallow breathing can be a reflection of poor health. Hashimoto recommended deep breathing or abdominal breathing exercises every day, particularly before bed.

Eating

Hashimoto recommended a simple macrobiotic diet, which in its original form was a wholegrain diet with small amounts of fish. Macrobiotics had been promoted by George Ohsawa and grew in popularity in the 1960s and 1970s. However, Hashimoto gave caution to being overzealous or strict in ones' diet and insisted that foods should be nourishing. He placed special emphasis on the importance of how well a food was chewed and digested rather than its quantity.

An important principle is that it is essential to have a balance of foods in the diet. Hashimoto considered it relevant that the design of our teeth consisted of molars for grinding nuts and grains, canines for cutting meat and front teeth for slicing fruits and vegetables. This composition implies that our diets should consist of these food groups in a ratio similar to our teeth composition. This variety of teeth types also suggests that extremes of diets such as pure vegetarianism or pure meat eating diets may not be in keeping with the natural state of man. A natural diet contains a proportion of meats, grains and vegetables. All as naturally grown as possible.

Movement

Movements that feel comfortable and can be carried out with ease are called *natural* movements. Abnormal movements which go against the natural state, place tension upon our muscles, joints and tendons causing structural and functional imbalances. If imbalances are present, sotai can help identify these imbalances and release them to restore the body's natural function and integrity.

Thought

Our thoughts, mindset and emotions interact and affect our physical body. A positive state of mind can keep us healthy. Conversely, feelings of contempt towards ourselves or against others, excess depression, sadness and anger can lead to an enervating effect upon our health and can inadvertently damage us.

Hashimoto considered our mindset to be as impactful as our breath. Our thoughts can make a good life or they can destroy us. Hashimoto suggested that we should not focus on upsetting events that we have no control over. Instead, to focus our thoughts on pleasant things as much as we can. To be grateful for what we have in life and avoid complaining.

Chapter Five: Reconnecting with our Bodies

"Our body is designed to live happily and healthily. Then why do we become sick? Because we live in a wrong way. We are breaking natural balance by wrong breathing, eating and drinking, body movement, and thinking.[1]*"*

Keizo Hashimoto

There are many factors that go against the natural way of life. For example, poor sanitation, unclean water, scarcity of food and pestilence were typical problems in the past and still affect developing countries today. In the modern age, there are many environmental substances that go against nature, such as pesticides and hormones in our meats and vegetables, microplastics and certain pharmaceuticals.

Other examples of wrong living include 'excesses'. These are excesses of stimulants like alcohol, tobacco, drugs and even food. Excesses of the emotions such as anger, sadness and fear, but also excess of activity and excitement, such as partying and gambling. An excess of work perversely can be a cause of disease. Take for example the phenomenon of *karoshi* in Japan, otherwise known as 'death by overwork'. In this situation, salaried workers work an unhealthy amount of overtime, which causes heart attacks, strokes or suicide. On the flip side, an excess of leisure and comfort has its downsides.

The human body living in a purely natural state can thrive in good health. We see examples of natural living versus unnatural living in animals. For example, the wood pigeon which lives in countryside areas are a bigger, more lustrous bird compared to its inner city relatives. Their diet is richer and healthier with leaves, fruits and berries. They live in trees surrounded by healthy green foliage. The air they breathe is clearer.

In contrast, the feral pigeon, a similar species to the wood pigeon, lives in city areas and is a smaller, weaker bird living solely on scraps of food left by city folk. Usually this is processed junk food full of sugar or processed oils. They live in crowded, dark, dusty tunnels surrounded by their own faeces. The air they breathe is polluted. They are seen as spreaders of disease. Some have deformed feet. It is also curious how city dwelling pigeons seem preoccupied with mating as much as possible, as though the unnatural lifestyle seems to foster excessive sexual desires.

Pet dogs and cats often suffer from similar illnesses that humans have, such as arthritis and cancer, which indicates that something about domestic and modern living is harmful to them. Zoo animals in captivity may show signs of mental apathy or illness.

Humans are the same. We are designed to move, use our bodies, to walk long distances, to be able to get on and off the floor easily, to have space, to have a close relationship to the earth and work on the land. Conversely, living in a state of heightened emotions, sitting in cars or at desks, stuffed away in cramped accommodation with limited space, being stressed about money or work and eating excessively is not a natural state for man.

Self-correction ability

There is an inbuilt sensitivity to physical imbalance present in all of us. It is our own internal red light dashboard display. Some people are more sensitive and react to it quickly, however some are less sensitive to disharmony and react slowly to it, only realising it until after they are sick.

One of the methods the body has to correct physical disharmonies is through unconscious actions or spontaneous movements such as yawning, crying or even talking to yourself. Moving during sleep can be a sign of correcting imbalances, which young children often do.

Healing

The philosophy of sotai is not focused on cure, but on encouraging the body's own self-healing. It is not as simple as 'do this exercise, and this problem will be cured'. Instead, it is a system of learning to listen to your body during practice and following the messages the body gives you. Hashimoto was aware of the limitations of medicine, with its objective to 'fix' the body the same way a person takes a car to a mechanic to 'fix' the problem. Hashimoto believed that it is not the therapist that does the healing. It is the body and its natural power that heals. The true therapist is one that supports this natural power.

Signs of dis-ease

Our body has ways of communicating to us its internal state. The first indicators of disharmony are abnormal sensations such as pain, dullness, numbness or stiffness. Next are physical signs affecting our organs, for example, an upset stomach, menstrual problems and so on. These symptoms usually prompt us to visit a doctor.

If we are in tune with nature, we may instinctively know how to heal. For example, cravings for foods when pregnant, are a sign that the body or the foetus needs something specific - a vitamin or mineral from that desired food. Some people naturally crave vegetables after a period of consuming only processed foods. However, we can lose these natural sensitivities by ignoring and overriding them and continuing to live in an unnatural way.

Movement system

Sotai self-healing exercises are based on the concept that our body moves as a whole – the muscles, the skeleton, cartilage, tendons, fascia, organs and skin. When one part of a body is used, other parts are involved. Diseases are a result of accumulation of deformations and incorrect movements.

Posture

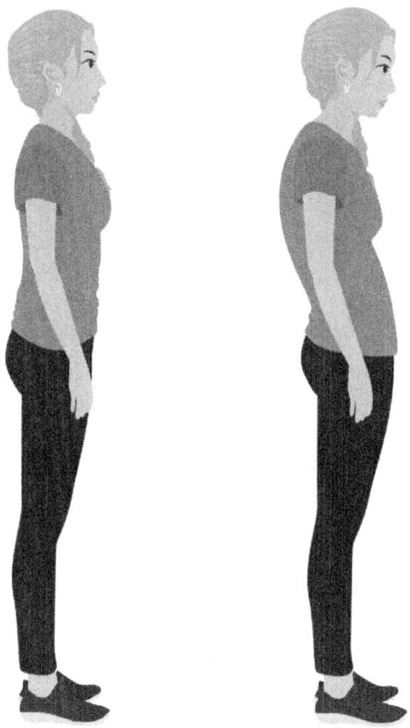

Image on left - good posture, body in balance. Image on right - imbalanced posture, slumped shoulders and hip tilted, indicates tightened muscles in pectorals, hamstrings, pelvis and back. What we don't see is how these shortened muscles impact on the internal organs within.

Abnormalities in the body show itself in the posture. Poor posture indicates muscles that are chronically tightened or shortened. Restoring the natural length of the muscles will take time and require regular movement of the affected areas. These muscles can be loosened by using natural and comfortable movements and encouraging them back into their natural resting length. As these shortened muscles are gradually corrected, the result will be a better posture and there may be an alleviation of pain and stiffness in the body.

The bodily ideal

Good posture means that the body operates in a state of efficient functioning. Poor postural habits can develop from many reasons, not just due to physical habits but also from emotional disharmony. For example, an excessive depressive state, apathy, poor self-esteem or feelings of inadequacy from childhood may lead to a head down and sunken chest habit. Excessive sitting or slumping, too much screen time, e.g. watching TV, playing video games, can create poor posture. Excessive eating and obesity can pull the natural posture out of alignment. Accidents, difficult childbirth and surgery can cause disfunctions. At an advanced stage, certain diseases such as cancer will affect the posture.

The body wants to achieve balance even in abnormality. However, if we try to force good posture where previously bad postural habits have consolidated, it can lead to pain, discomfort and fatigue. The body will typically adapt to a posture that is out of alignment and make it function as efficiently as it can. This has its downsides as well as it advantages. The advantage being that a person can continue functioning, working and carrying out life as required. This can go on for many years. The downside is that it is not operating in a state of peak efficiency and these imbalances become entrenched.

Gravity centre

The pelvis is the base of all movements. One important concept in traditional Japanese arts is that there should be a synergy of the movement of hands and feet with that of the pelvis. The centre of gravity should be based on the centre line of the body. This concept finds its expression in a multitude of traditional Japanese arts such as karate, kendo and even tea ceremony. Ideally, we stand with our weight focused on the centre of the ball of the feet area. This focuses the centre of gravity onto the centre line.

Additionally, movement emanates from the hara (a point in the lower abdomen), which also incorporates the area known as the *koshi* (hips) and is said to be the base of movement and power. This expression can be recognised in activities like boxing where a powerful punch emanates from the hips, the lower back, the legs and then through the arms and fists. Or baseball when the hips and waist must activate first before swinging the bat. This movement brings unity of the body.

The centre of balance can be off for some people. This occurs naturally when a person favours one side over the other. A right handed person will naturally favour the right side in carrying out exercises. Potentially, this may lead to minute skeletal imbalances such as having one leg appearing to be longer than the other. This imbalance can be noticed when lying with legs side by side on a flat surface.

This is one of the reasons why activities like yoga usually perform exercises on the left and right sides of the body so as to keep the sides equally balanced. The Chinese system of qigong also involves standing with feet equally balanced and focusing on the hara (lower abdomen).

Movement should be balanced or distributed between the right and left sides of the body. To give an example, if you are right handed and you are picking up a pencil from the floor, a common habit will be to step forward with the right foot, bend over and pick up the object with the right hand. This places the centre of gravity more to the right side. Over time, if this movement and habit is repeated, the centre of balance will be set more unequally on the right side causing subtle stresses on the body and spinal alignment.

Instead step forward with the left foot, bend and reach with the right hand. This movement creates better body alignment and naturally feels more comfortable.

An example of this principle in sports is the pool or snooker player. A right handed player will typically position their left foot forwards and their left hand in front on the table. Their right hand is the trigger hand for shooting the pot. Try doing the same pose but instead have the right foot forward and it will feel naturally wrong.

With movement, we typically walk and swing our arms for gentle momentum. The right leg moves forward and the left arm swings forward. The left leg moves forward and the right arm swings forward. This is the natural rhythm. If we disturb this rhythm by putting the right arm forward with the right foot, it would look and feel unnatural. Even simply walking with our hands in our pockets, may lead to small micro imbalances as it disturbs our natural rhythm.

Overuse

Overusing or overtraining a particular muscle or joint such as when training for sports or a specific occupation can lead to stiffness or pain in that part of the body. For example a healthcare worker or furniture remover who suffers from back pain from repeated lifting, or a sportsperson or musician with a pain in their elbow from overperforming a specific action. These people have to learn to mitigate the risks of their profession and find ways to avoid overstressing these areas.

Sickness

Sickness can result when the way of life has fallen significantly out of order and the body has failed to adapt. A mental, emotional, physical or environmental stress, which has gone beyond the body's capacity to deal with it.

Imbalances cause stress which affects the muscles and fascia layers subtly. Maladjusted muscles harden or fix into patterns of tension, affecting the joints, the circulatory system and nervous system. The first signs of abnormalities in the body may be pain, malaise, tiredness or indistinct symptoms. If these imbalances progress, they may start to affect the internal organs. In this case, a specific disease could be diagnosed. Some imbalances can still be reversed, but if they go past a certain point, it is harder for the body to correct itself and instead invasive medical interventions and pharmaceuticals may be required.

Hashimoto wrote that a faulty way of thinking is to focus on curing "such and such disease" or to consider that a person is sick because such and such organ is diseased. It is far better to say "*my organs are unhealthy because my body is unhealthy*". In Western medicine, the damaged or malfunctioning organ is seen as the primary cause of disease. There is usually no explanation as to why it is malfunctioning. Sometimes, a reason is given such as perhaps it runs in the family or it may be *genetic*. However, in sotai, damaged organs are not the original cause of illness. The damaged organs are caused by deformation in the body. Western medicine will focus on healing the damaged part first. Sotai aims to correct the original imbalances.

Correcting deformation

The natural state of our bodies is to feel good. People often misuse their bodies taking for granted the health and resilience they have. The natural state of health is similar to having the body of a child again, before imbalances have been created. However, years of maladaptation and maladjustment will cause our body to become distorted. The body in its wisdom adapts to these maladaptations and makes each deformation as comfortable as possible. We become so used to these deformations that if we were by magic to be returned to a natural healthy state - perhaps the body of a child again, it would feel alien to us. Can you imagine how lighter and looser a child's body must be compared to a middle-aged person? Additionally, we get used to our own unique imbalances so that if another person was to be magically transplanted into our body they would probably groan in discomfort at the restrictions they would experience for the first time. As the years progress, these imbalances become so entrenched as a part of us, we don't notice them anymore.

Chapter Six: Sotai Body Self-Assessment

A key principle of sotai is to avoid painful movements. In sotai, you make movements of the body into the direction that feels comfortable. In this way, sotai has the benefit of rehabilitating the area without aggravating the condition. Breathing is also a factor. Movements should be carried out on an exhale, not an inhale. However, this rule can be relaxed if it is too difficult to carry out.

We can assess for imbalances or deformations in our bodies by observing the range of movement and our posture to identify where tensions and restrictions exist. This involves assessing the movement of your joints, your hips and waist, upper body, limbs and spine.

We can check for imbalances by moving our joints in a relaxed way, within their natural range of movement. For example, left and right, back and forth, contracting and then relaxing. For example, with our hand we can move it to the left and right, we can clench our hand into a fist and then release it. We can flex the wrist and then extend it, twist it to one side and then the other. We can move it in a circular direction clockwise and anticlockwise. It is notable that these motions are similar to the wrist warm-up exercises used in martial arts.

Similar exercises can be carried out on different joints in the body – the neck, the elbows, the knees and the ankles. These exercises not only encourage suppleness but also help prevent injuries if done regularly.

If when carrying out any of these exercises, we identify problem areas – joints that are stiff, painful or difficult to move in certain directions, we can see examples of deformations. There may be instances where joints are clinically malformed. For example, osteoarthritis where the knotty deposits have hardened. In these cases, the deformations have set and sotai should be practiced cautiously, as there is a possibility of aggravating the pain. Nonetheless, some kind of daily movement may be beneficial to the affected joints. Arthritis in early stages can benefit from gentle movements.

Posture assessment

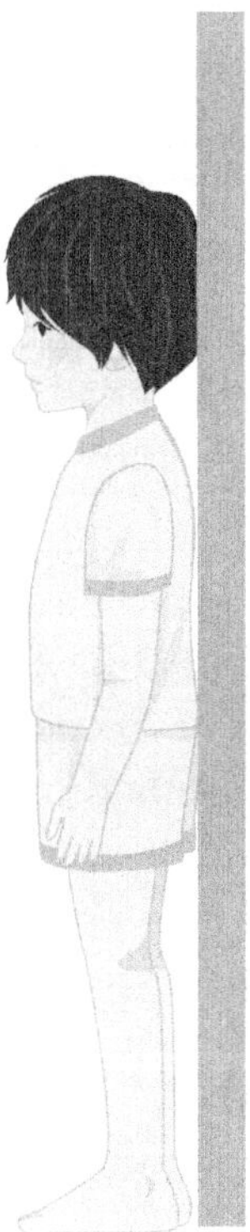

Children have naturally good posture when carrying out the wall assessment

Our posture provides an immediate indication of the state of our body. A simple postural assessment can be carried out against the wall.

Stand with your back against a wall. The back of the feet about one inch away from the wall. Touch your bottom, the upper part of your back and the back of your head against the wall as much as your body allows. Do not touch the back of the feet against the wall. You should be able to insert a hand between the small of the back (lower back) and the wall. Simply hold this pose for a few seconds and see how it feels. Does it feel comfortable? Is it natural? Do you have to force yourself to maintain this position?

For some people, this will feel uncomfortable. The more discomfort you feel indicates the more out of balance your posture is. Take note of which areas feel less comfortable.

If you are relatively comfortable in this position, it indicates your body is in a more balanced state. Young people, especially children will find this pose relatively comfortable as their bodies are closer to the ideal state and they have not yet been distorted by years of unnatural living and poor body habits.

Feet

Correcting the posture starts from correcting the feet. It is possible to check for postural imbalances by checking the condition of shoes that have been well worn in and comparing left and right. For example, if one side is more worn away than the other, then we can see a disharmony between the right and left sides of our body, possibly a hip imbalance. The ideal pattern is where both shoes are worn down equally.

Modern footwear is unnatural for our feet and are designed for a flat, hard surface. Heals on shoes, both for men and women, throw our centre of gravity forward. Even thick socks soften and weaken our feet.

However, if a person has spent a lifetime wearing heeled shoes or trainers, any sudden change to more simple footwear can result in pains in the lower legs and feet. Any changes to walking habits or footwear should be introduced gradually to allow the body to adapt.

Sandals or flat shoes, with a minimal sole are more natural than cushioned trainers or stiff leather shoes with heels.

Sitting

Being able to sit comfortably on the floor tells us much about our physical state. There are two optimal ways of sitting – cross-legged and the Japanese seiza pose, with knees bent and feet folded under the legs.

Typically children can sit in relative ease in either posture, though ‘use it or lose it’ applies, and if they do not practice regularly, these postures become harder. Unfortunately, it is common for adults, especially in the West, to find both poses difficult to sit in. Common issues are pins and needles, but also joint pain and for others it is simply no longer possible to move their legs into position. By their very nature, these poses require a person to get on and off the floor, which is also an activity a person may struggle with.

Seiza sitting

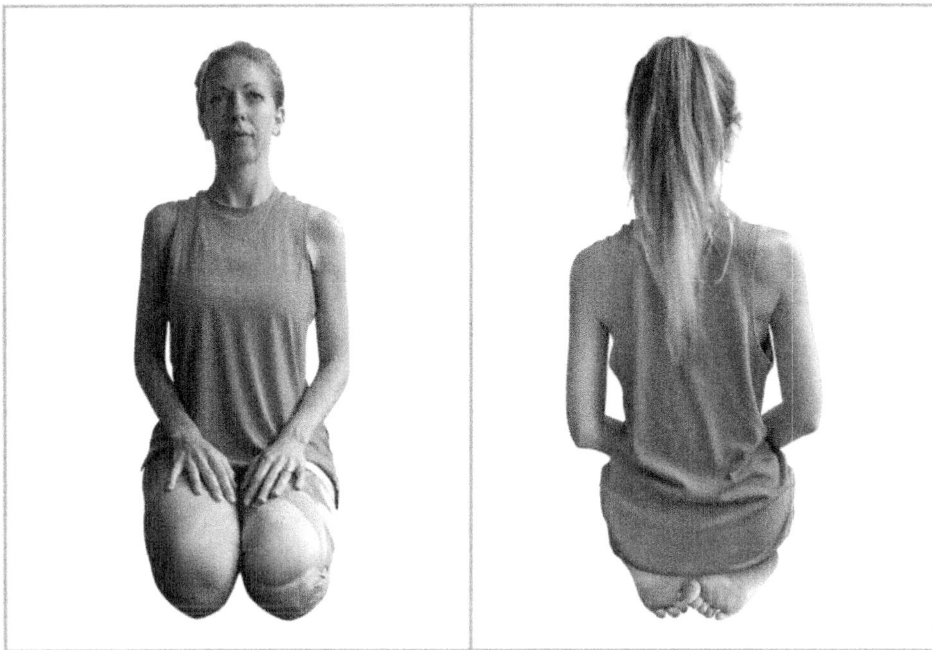

This is a good sitting exercise to improve your posture. If you fatigue easily in this position or cannot hold a straight back, it indicates tightness in your pelvic region and weakness in your spinal muscles. It is recommended to try and sit a few minutes a day and build up to longer periods. Your legs will likely go numb, so be prepared to take a break and move them to get the circulation back.

Posture and emotions

Our emotional state is reflected in our bodily posture. Our postural habits also can influence our emotional state. There is a strong correlation between specific emotions and our physical health in traditional Chinese medicine. Bodyworkers observe that specific body holding patterns correspond to certain emotional states.

Chapter Seven: How Sotai Works – A Scientific Explanation

In research carried out at Waseda University in Tokyo[2], sotai was studied and summarised as:

> *Performance of movements that feel good will bring improvement in movements that are painful. Specifically, a person moves their body in a different direction to the pain to identify the movement that feels good. Then they slowly breathe out and carry on performing movements in the directions that feel good. Hold the position for a few seconds or until tired and repeat the same movements. By doing so, the movements that feel painful should improve.*

The scientific rationale for this working, is because patients who suffer chronic pain are typically experiencing deformations in the anatomical and functional aspects of their muscular skeletal system. Self-amplification of pain is continuously switched on. Any stimulation of the deformed muscle areas causes stimulation of pain messages as well as agitation to the sympathetic nerves and constriction of blood supply causing poor circulation of blood and oxygen to the affected muscles. This then results in further amplification of the pain sensation. Additionally due to reduced circulation, other pain inducing substances and metabolites which cause pain, accumulate in the affected area, making the pain and restriction worse.

In these situations, two sets of muscles are involved. These are muscles that contract to carry out the movements and other muscles that relax - otherwise known as the antagonistic muscle pair.

Typically conventional rehabilitation involves movement of the affected muscle in the direction of pain, e.g. stretching to ensure that the patient does not fall into a cycle of self-amplifying pain (or chronic pain), though this involves having to tolerate a small amount of pain.

However, sotai works in the opposite way to this by finding movements that do not cause pain and by moving in those directions in order to rehabilitate the areas that are in pain. This is a safer method as there is no aggravation of the deformity.

Performing the sotai movement that feels pleasant with the gentle contraction of the muscle and small amount of tension, followed by relaxing the movement, will improve the blood flow and thus allow rehabilitation of the antagonistic muscle, which may be the source of pain.

Part II

二

How to do Sotai

The purpose of the basic sotai exercises is to slowly rehabilitate the joints and muscles of the body, correct imbalances and help prevent injuries. They can also be used diagnostically. If pain or stiffness is felt with any of these particular exercises, it indicates an unbalanced area to be worked on further.

In the next section, we will cover the basic sotai exercises, but before we go on, there are some simple guidance points.

Basic Guide on movement

A key concept is that if there is any discomfort or pain in the body, avoid moving into the uncomfortable direction. Instead identify the movement that feels good and move into this direction.

The tendency for a person with muscle pain is to point out where it hurts and be drawn to that area. Instead you need to find the movement, where not only does it not hurt, but it feels good to move in that direction. This is the rehabilitative direction.

If there are no areas of pain in the body, then be aware of restrictions or tightness in the movements, especially between the right and left sides of the body or when moving in specific directions. Then focus on moving into the direction of ease and comfort.

When the direction that feels comfortable is identified, slowly breathe out and carry on performing the movements in that *good* direction. Hold for a few seconds, or repeat the movement. Gradually, the painful side will improve by working on the good side.

Identifying the comfortable and uncomfortable direction

Take each exercise slowly. Be aware of which side feels comfortable and which does not. Find the side or movement that elicits pain, is tight or has any other kind of uncomfortable sensation. Then compare it with the opposite side or find another direction that feels good.

Do more repetitions in that comfortable direction. At the end, try the uncomfortable direction again to see if there is any change in the pain or level of restriction.

Some of the exercises are general rebalancing movements. Other exercises contain an aspect of comparing different sides or directions with instructions to place more emphasis on working on the comfortable side. Take care with every movement and be respectful of your body.

If any exercises are too difficult or painful to perform, it is permissible to miss them out. Work on the exercises that you can do. You can always revisit some of these exercises later on to see if anything has changed.

On repetitions

The instructions that follow are a starting guide. However, they should not be seen as rigid rules. As Hashimoto developed his system, he realised that rules about repetitions and breathing should not be fixed, but should be based on how the body feels when carrying out the movements. In practice, consider the number that works for you or let the body tell you how many you should do by what feels *right* and whether further repetitions are desired by the body. This takes it away from being a fixed system into a responsive way of learning to listen to the body.

A note on breathing normally

In, sotai, it was originally taught that when movement stops, inhale and then slowly exhale during movement. The reason for this is that during exhalation, the body is in a more relaxed state so there is less tension when you perform the movement.

However, strictly following this guidance may not be right for everyone. In regards to breathing, a healthy person may feel it easy to move during the exhalation. However a person with bodily imbalances, may find their breathing pattern hindered and find it uncomfortable to exhale on the movement.

Sometimes, the bodily distortions have created a balance in the body where shallow breathing helps the body to function. Making a person who has been a shallow breather for several years, start to do deep breathing could be detrimental to them resulting in light-headedness or dizziness. In these cases, just breathing normally (to them), when carrying out the movements is better, without trying to control the breath. If you find the inhalations and exhalations too difficult to coordinate, it is permissible to breathe as normal during the exercises.

These basic sotai exercises are an excellent regiment to add to your daily practice. They can be done first thing in the morning or at night before bed. They help to keep your body supple and in good condition. As they are gentle and low impact, they can be practiced by people of all ages and at different states of fitness.

The Sotai Self-Exercises

操体法

Exercise 1.

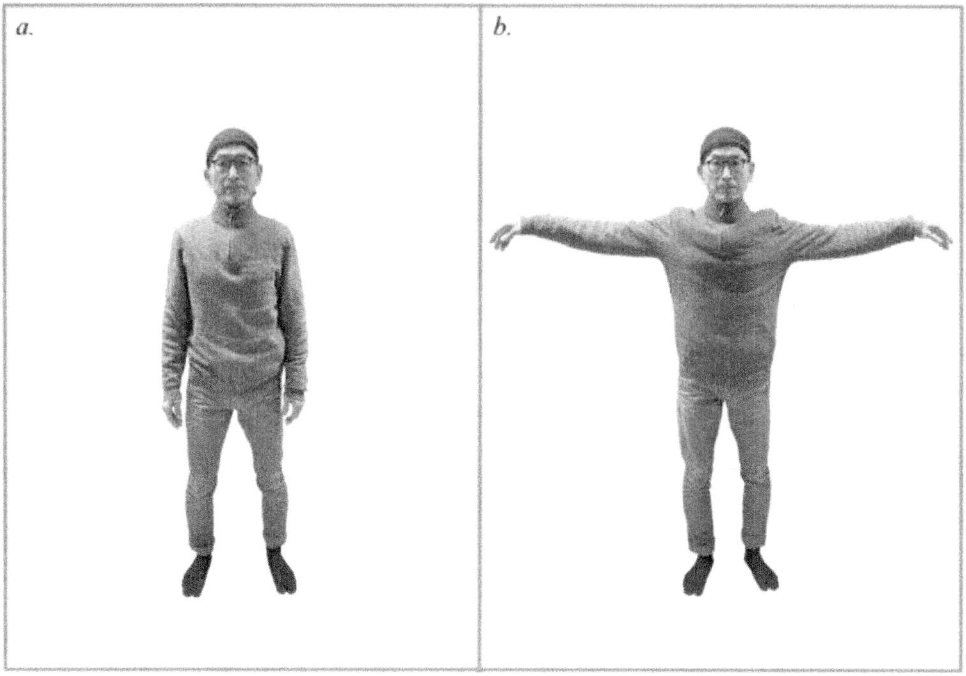

This exercise rebalances the shoulders.

Instructions

Stand with feet shoulder-width apart. Keep your back straight. Look ahead. Inhale, and then as you exhale, raise your arms straight out from the sides till they are level in a 'T' shape.

Inhale and hold your breath for a count of three. Then exhale quickly and as you do so, let your arms drop down quickly to the starting position by the side of the body. Do this exercise three to five times.

You can breathe normally when carrying out the movements, but do aim to drop your arms on an exhalation.

Exercise 2.

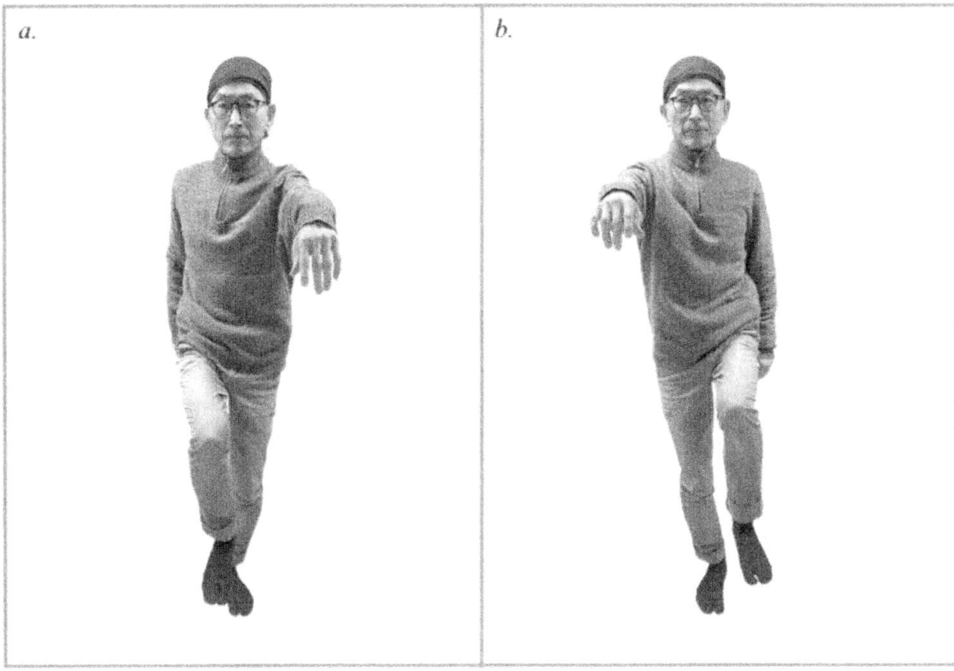

This helps to recalibrate your left and right coordination.

Instructions

This is like marching on the spot. Stand with feet together. Raise your right leg till your thigh is parallel to the ground. Keep your foot pointing downwards. Raise the arm on the opposite side of the body to shoulder level. Allow the right arm to swing slightly backwards. Then put the foot back down to the ground quickly.

Do the other side, lift the left leg and raise the right arm accordingly. Put your foot down to the ground quickly.

Change sides again. Repeat this movement thirty to fifty times. You can breathe normally during the movements if it is preferable.

Exercise 3.

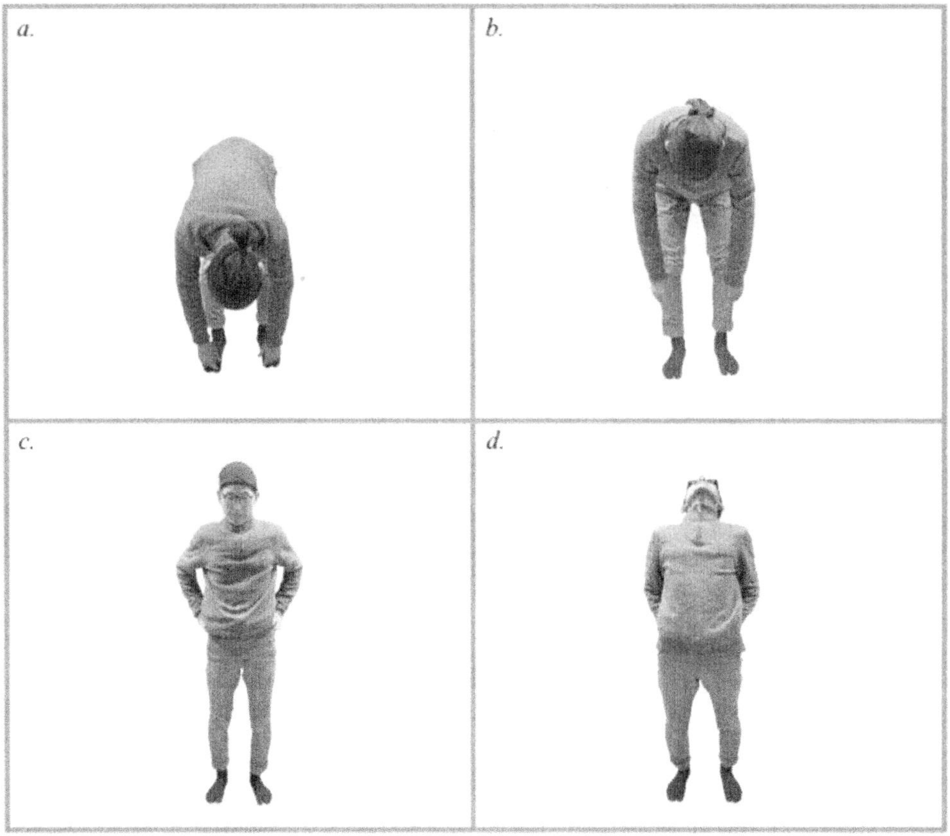

This invigorates and stretches the front and back of the body, especially the lower back and the abdomen.

Instructions

Stand with feet hip-width apart. Inhale, then as you exhale, bend forward from the waist, let the arms drop forward to the ground.

Inhale, then on a slow exhale raise your head and lift your upper body to the upright position. Put your hands on the back of your hips to support your lower back and slightly bend backwards. Let your head drop backwards.

Inhale quickly and when you exhale bring your body back to the initial starting position. Then repeat the exercise three to five times.

You can breathe normally during the movements if it is preferable.

Exercise 4.

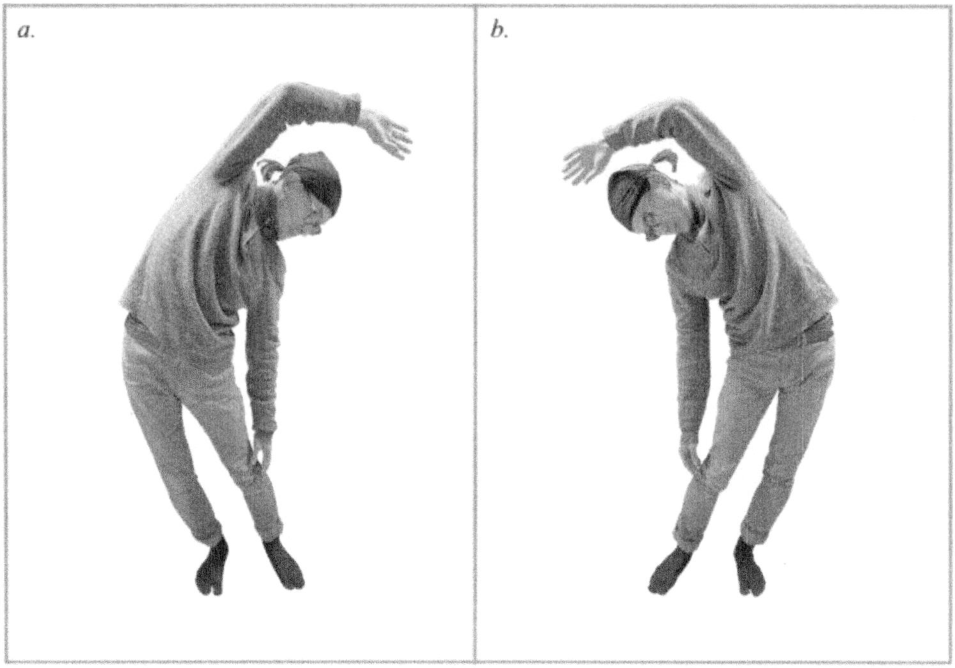

This exercise helps balance the left and right sides of the body.

Instructions

Stand with feet hip-width apart. Put your left hand on your waist and push your hips outwards to the right side. Inhale, then as you slowly exhale, raise your right arm over your head and reach over to the left side. Inhale, then as you exhale slowly bring your arm back to the side.

Then repeat the exercise on the opposite side. Do each side three to five times. If you notice that one side is easier than the other, do the easy side one to two more times and then one more time on the harder side.

You can breathe normally during the movements if it is preferable.

Exercise 5.

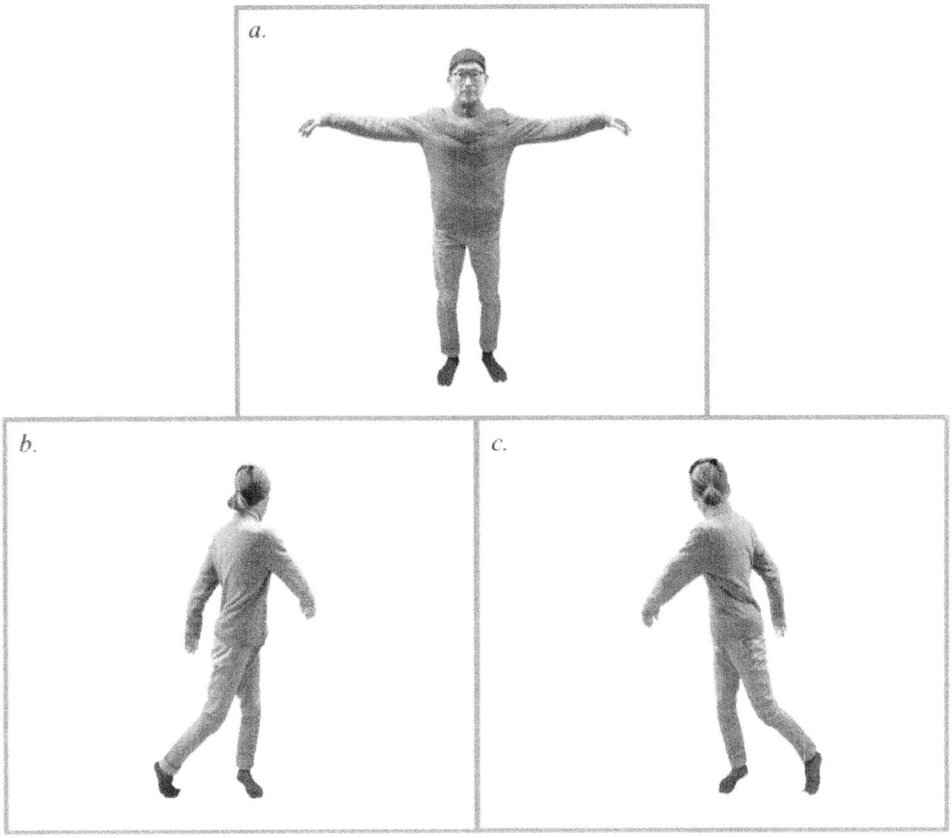

This exercise is beneficial for the waist and spinal column. It involves a slow twisting motion.

Instructions

Stand with feet hip-width apart. Extend your arms out to the sides. Inhale, then as you exhale, slowly turn your body to the left and look over your left shoulder. As you do so, keep your left foot flat on the ground, but allow your right heel to raise off the ground. Aim to keep your arms up while you turn. Inhale, then as you exhale, bring your arms and body back to the starting position.

Repeat on the opposite side. Do the exercise three to five times on both sides. If one side has more tension than the other, do two to three more times on the easier side and one more time on the difficult side.

Breathe normally during the movements if it is preferable.

Exercise 6.

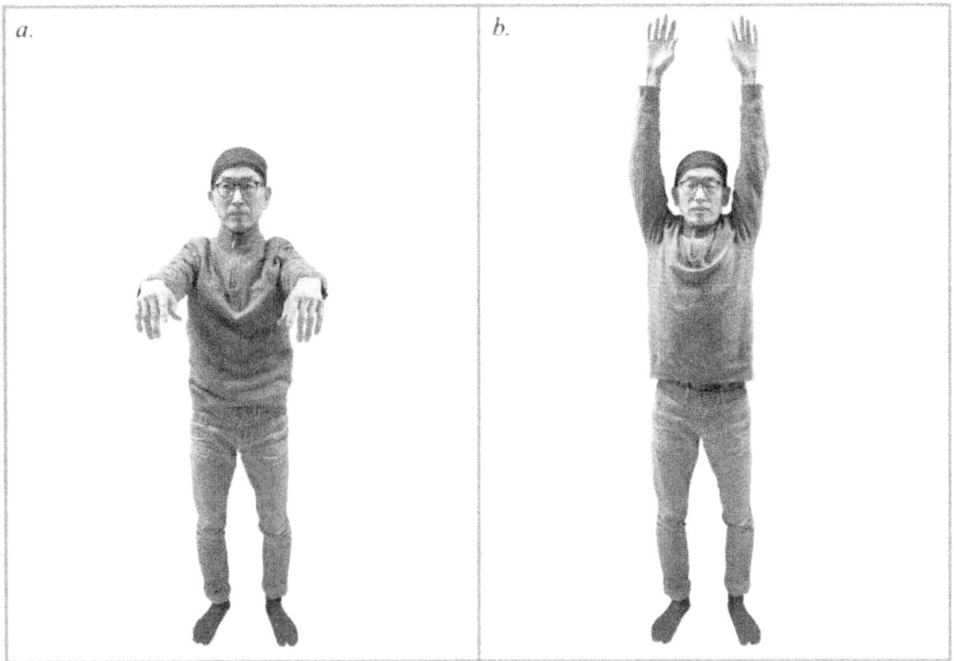

This works on the entire skeletal structure.

Instructions

Stand with feet hip-width apart. Breathe in, then as you exhale, raise your arms up from the front and reach to the sky. Lift your heels off the ground and stand on tiptoe. Inhale. Hold your breath for a count of three. Then exhale quickly dropping your heels and arms back to the starting position. Repeat this exercise three to five times.

Breathe normally during the movements if it is preferable, but aim to drop your heels on an exhalation.

Exercise 7.

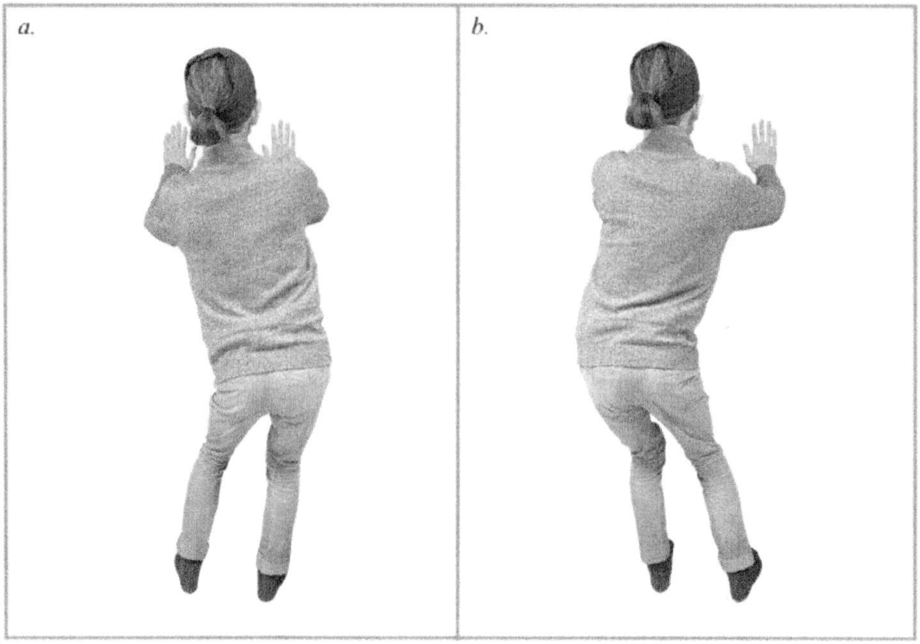

This exercise helps to balance the waist, thighs and lower back.

Instructions

Stand facing a wall, feet hip-width apart. Extend your arms and touch the wall. Then bend your knees as low as is comfortable.

Breathe in, then slowly exhale and move your hips to the right and then to the left. Come back to the centre and then repeat the exercise going in the opposite direction – left to right, then centre.

Do this exercise three to five times. If one direction is more uncomfortable, do the exercise in the easier direction two more times and then one more time on the challenging side. Breathe normally during the movements if it is preferable.

Exercise 8.

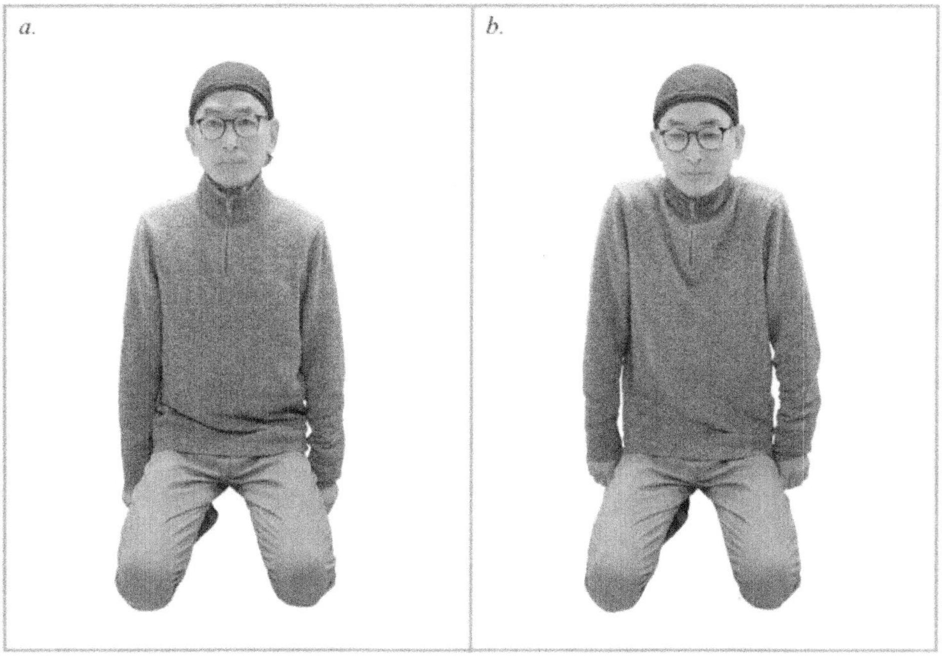

This exercise incorporates the sitting seiza pose - a traditional way of sitting in Japan. It helps release tension in the shoulders.

Instructions

Sit in seiza pose. Your knees are bent and legs folded under your bottom. If you are right handed, keep your right big toe over the left big toe. If left handed, left big toe over the right toe. You can keep your knees close together or apart, about one hands-width, depending on what feels comfortable. If the seiza position is not comfortable, this pose can be done either cross-legged or in a chair. It is important to keep the back straight and spine upright.

Inhale, then slowly exhale raising your shoulders to your ears. Inhale. Hold your breath for a count of three and then exhale quickly dropping your shoulders at the same time. Repeat this exercise three to five times. Breathe normally during the movements but aim to drop your shoulders on an exhalation.

Exercise 9.

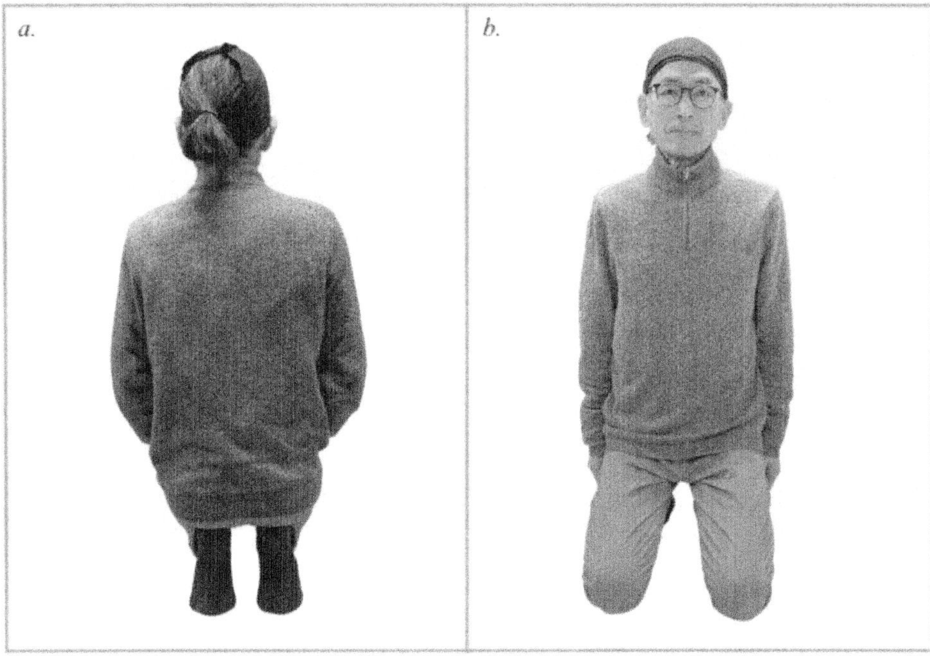

Instructions

Sit down on the floor. Put your knees together and sit on your heels with toes pressing into the floor. Put your hands on your heels.

Inhale, then as you exhale, slowly bend your torso forward. Move your upper body in a circle to the right side, then to the back. At the back, inhale again and as you exhale, continue circling to the left side, then back to the front.

Repeat the exercise two more times in the same direction and then change and move in the opposite direction three times.

Breathe normally during the movements if it is preferable.

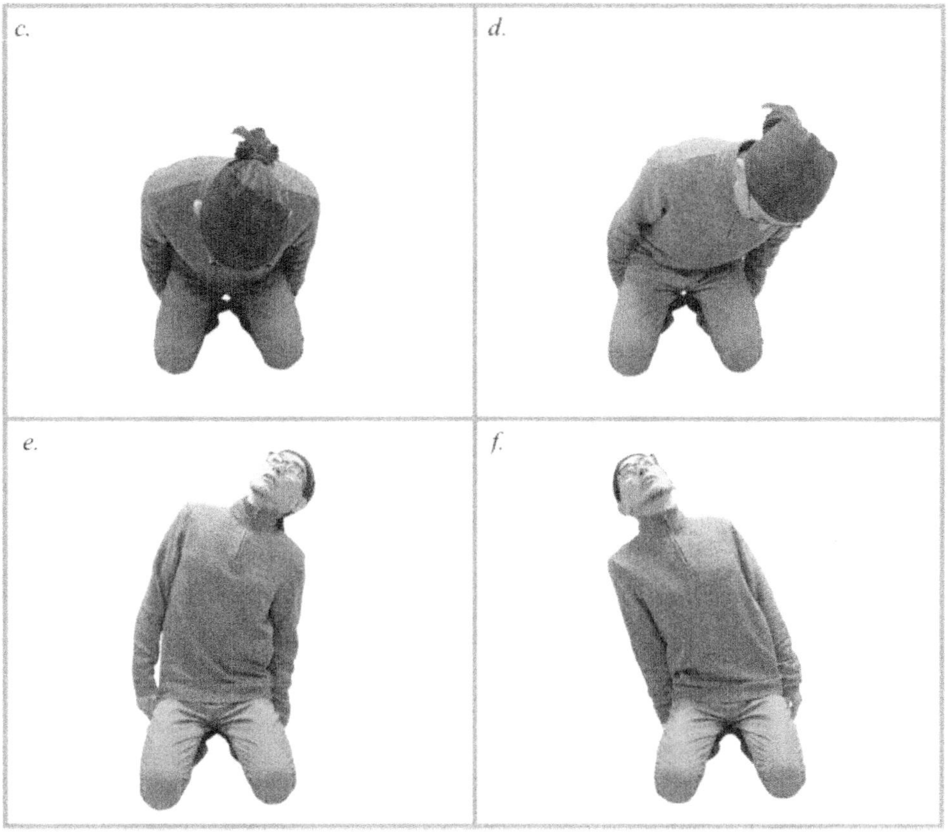

This exercise involves circling the upper body in a seated position. This helps strengthen the ankles and stretches the feet and toes. It helps rebalance the waist, spine and back.

Exercise 10.

This pose recalibrates the hips, shoulders and spine. It is based on the movement of a four-legged animal. It has three stages.

Instructions

Put your knees and hands on the floor in the pose of an animal. Find the centre position. This is your starting position. You can breathe normally during the movements.

First move your hips to the left and to the right. Then back to the centre.

Then move your shoulders to the left and right. Then back to the centre.

Finally, move your body forward and then backwards.

Repeat the sequence three to five times.

Exercise 11.

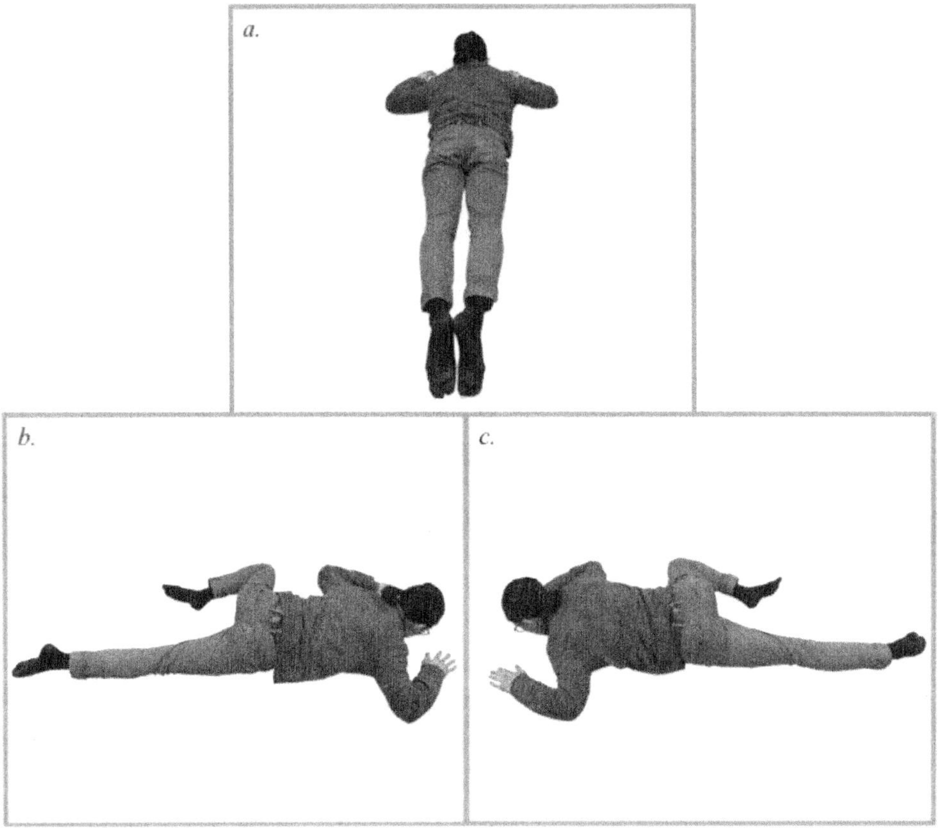

This exercise opens up the front of the hips and thighs - an area which commonly becomes tight and can be implicated in problems involving the digestive or gynaecological system. It is similar to the way a crocodile crawls along the ground, though you do not move forward when carrying out this exercise.

Instructions

Lie on the floor on your abdomen. Place your hands under your head to support it with palms facing downwards. Turn your head to the left and bring your left knee up as far as is comfortable. Inhale, then as you exhale return your knee back to its starting position.

Repeat the exercise on the other side. Turn your head to the right, and move your right knee up as far as is comfortable. Inhale, then as you exhale, move your knee back to its starting position.

Do both sides three to five times. If one side feels more difficult, do the easier side two more times, and then do the hard side one last time.

Breathe normally during the movements if it is preferable.

Exercise 12a.

Exercises 12a. and 12b. helps balance the wrists and hands. They are both carried out in seiza pose which is beneficial for your posture.

Instructions

Sit in seiza. Keep a straight back. Clap your hands twenty times.

Exercise 12b.

This exercise involves shaking the wrists and hands. It helps keep the wrists supple.

Instructions

Sit in seiza. Shake your hands vigorously fifteen times.

Instructions for carrying out sotai exercises

There are several exercises listed here. Try all the exercises to assess those you find easy, those that are difficult and those that feel good. Exercises which are uncomfortable can indicate specific areas of deformation or imbalance. In this case, it may be beneficial to work on those particular exercises but pay special attention to moving into the comfortable direction as per sotai guidelines and avoid the painful directions. If after regularly practicing these exercises, they become easier, it is a sign that the imbalance is being improved.

Due to time constraints, it may be advisable to pick two or three exercises to practice in a session. It is good to get into the habit of practicing first thing in the morning or last thing at night.

As mentioned earlier, if the instructions for breathing, particularly the inhale and exhale, is too difficult to follow, then the exercises can be carried out with normal breathing. Also, the number of repetitions can be adjusted to suit you, but make sure not to overdo them. More repetitions does not mean fixing the body quicker.

Move away from ego

Movement in sotai should not be based on ego or desire. It is based on the internal bodily awareness of what feels right and it is about connecting to your body. Let go the desire for a 'fix' or cure which can be a distraction.

These exercises are given as an introductory guide to sotai. There are other types of movement and at a higher level, your body can even guide you into what movement it needs to do to correct itself. In doing your own practice, you may find a movement, not described in this book, which you are driven to practice. The question to ask yourself is - does this movement feel right? Does your body want more of this movement? If the answer is yes, this is sotai.

Conclusion

Lessons of the body

Sotai is a way of learning to access the body as a teacher. Movements that feel *right*, should be seen as the body instructing you what it needs to correct itself. Movements that feel *wrong*, which feel uncomfortable or even painful, is the body telling you that these movements will exacerbate the problem or hinder healing and to avoid these movements.

The lesson is simply to follow what the body teaches. In Christianity, the teachings of which influenced Hashimoto's early life, God gave man *free will*. Likewise, we have free will to listen to our bodies or to ignore them. Listening can lead to healing. Ignoring can lead to suffering.

Healing is not just about fixing the body or seeking a cure. Healing and treatment provides a chance to reflect on what we are doing wrong in our lives. This is especially the case when a person is ill and must spend a period of time convalescing. Sickness provides an opportunity for spiritual growth. A period of rest following sickness can lead to a greater relationship with our bodies. Especially, if previously we had an abusive relationship with it, taking it for granted by eating, thinking and living in unnatural ways.

Hashimoto recognised that there is a link between the body structure, its mechanics and the health of the body. Imbalances occur when we do not live in a state natural to man. Healing can occur if we can recognise and correct our unnatural way of living. All we require is to increase our knowledge. Taking more control of our bodies so that we can live and function better is the *sotai* way.

References

[1]Sotai Natural Exercise. Hashimoto, Keizo, M.D. Translated by Aihara, Herman. George Ohsawa Macrobiotic Foundation. Chico, California. 1981.

[2]Promoting Bilateral Symmetry in the Body through an Eastern Medical Approach Examining the Chaotic Nature of Pulse Waves Using a Neck Rotation Task via Sotai Therapy. Takikawa, Ryoko & Ishii, Yasumoto. International Journal of Electronics and Communication Engineering and Technology (IJECET). Volume 7, Issue 3, May-June 2016.

Bibliography

Sotai Treatment Room: Obeying Bodily Sensations. Standard edition, Miura, Hiroshi. 2016.

Printed in Dunstable, United Kingdom

75549115R00040